Itty Bitty Animals

ITTY BITTY GECKOS

By T. H. Baer

Gareth Stevens Publishing

Please visit our website, www.garethstevens.com. For a free color catalog of all our high-quality books, call toll free 1-800-542-2595 or fax 1-877-542-2596.

Library of Congress Cataloging-in-Publication Data

Baer, T.H.
Itty bitty geckos / by T.H. Baer.
p. cm. — (Itty bitty animals)
Includes index.
ISBN 978-1-4339-9880-5 (pbk.)
ISBN 978-1-4339-9881-2 (6-pack)
ISBN 978-1-4339-9878-2 (library binding)
1. Geckos — Juvenile literature. I. Title.
QL666.L245 B34 2014
597.952—dc23

First Edition

Published in 2014 by
Gareth Stevens Publishing
111 East 14th Street, Suite 349
New York, NY 10003

Editor: Ryan Nagelhout
Designer: Nicholas Domiano

Photo credits: Cover, p.1 © iStockphoto.com/NKW-Photography; p. 5 Comstock/Thinkstock.com; p. 7 Evgeniy Ayupov/Shutterstock.com; p. 9 Christian Colista/Shutterstock.com p. 11 reptiles4all/Shutterstock.com; p. 13 Arto Hakola/Shutterstock.com; p. 15 Anastasiia Lieonova/Shutterstock.com; p. 17 iStockphoto/Thinkstock.com; p. 19 ROBERTO ZILLI/Shutterstock.com; pp. 21, 24 (tail) Micha Fleuren/Shutterstock.com; p. 23 alslutsky/ Shutterstock.com; p. 24 (rocks) yotrak/Shutterstock.com.

Printed in the United States of America

CPSIA compliance information: Batch #CW14GS: For further information contact Gareth Stevens, New York, New York at 1-800-542-2595.

Contents

Geckos are tiny!

They are a kind of small lizard.

There are over 1,000 kinds!

They are many different colors.

Some look like trees or rocks. This helps them hide.

Others are very bright. This keeps away animals that eat them.

Geckos lick their eyes to clean them.

They like to climb up walls.

Geckos can lose their tail. They can even grow a new one!

They store fat
in their tail.

Words to Know

rocks

tail

Index